Violin Grade 4

Pieces
for Trinity College London examinations

2010-2015

Published by:
Trinity College London
89 Albert Embankment
London SE1 7TP UK

T +44 (0)20 7820 6100
F +44 (0)20 7820 6161
E music@trinitycollege.co.uk
www.trinitycollege.co.uk

Registered in England
Company no. 02683033
Charity no. 1014792

Copyright © 2009 Trinity College London
Fifth impression, April 2014

Unauthorised photocopying is illegal
No part of this publication may be copied or reproduced in any
form or by any means without the prior permission of the publisher.

Music processed by New Notations London and Moira Roach.
Printed in England by Halstan, Amersham, Bucks.

GROUP A

Giga

Joseph Boulogne, le chevalier de Saint-George
(1745-1799)

Dynamics are editorial.

GROUP A

Menuet and Trio

Jules Danbé
(1840-1905)

GROUP A

Mosquito Dance
op. 62 no. 5

Ludwig Mendelssohn
(1855-1933)

For this piece the printed fingering must be used in the examination.

ed. Barbara Barber. Copyright © 1997 SUMMY-BIRCHARD MUSIC, a division of SUMMY-BIRCHARD, INC.
Exclusive Print Rights Administered by ALFRED MUSIC PUBLISHING. All Rights Reserved. Used by Permission.

Lean Mean Tango

Mary Cohen

Copyright © 2006 by Faber Music Ltd, London.
Reproduced from *First Repertoire for Violin* by permission of the publishers.

Waltz

from *Album for the Young* op. 39 no. 8

Pyotr Ilyich Tchaikovsky
(1840–1893)

Violin Grade 4

Pieces
for Trinity College London examinations

2010-2015

Published by:
Trinity College London
89 Albert Embankment
London SE1 7TP UK

T +44 (0)20 7820 6100
F +44 (0)20 7820 6161
E music@trinitycollege.co.uk
www.trinitycollege.co.uk

Registered in England
Company no. 02683033
Charity no. 1014792

Copyright © 2009 Trinity College London
Fifth impression, April 2014

Unauthorised photocopying is illegal
No part of this publication may be copied or reproduced in any form or by any means without the prior permission of the publisher.

Music processed by New Notations London and Moira Roach.
Printed in England by Halstan, Amersham, Bucks.

TG 008268
ISBN 978-0-85736-062-5

GROUP A

Prelude

Mary Cohen

(1) Blocked fifth: prepare the chord by placing 1st finger across 2 strings before playing.
This piece is played unaccompanied in the examination.

Copyright © 1992 by Faber Music Ltd, London.
Reproduced from *Technique Takes Off!* (*Violin*) by permission of the publishers.

Giga

Joseph Boulogne, le chevalier de Saint-George
(1745–1799)

GROUP A

Mosquito Dance
op. 62 no. 5

Ludwig Mendelssohn
(1855-1933)

For this piece the printed fingering must be used in the examination.

ed. Barbara Barber. Copyright © 1997 SUMMY-BIRCHARD MUSIC, a division of SUMMY-BIRCHARD, INC.
Exclusive Print Rights Administered by ALFRED MUSIC PUBLISHING. All Rights Reserved. Used by Permission.

GROUP B

Waltz
from *Album for the Young* op. 39 no. 8

Pyotr Ilyich Tchaikovsky
(1840–1893)

GROUP B

Flor de Yumuri

arr. Edward Huw Jones

Jorge Anckermann
(1877–1941)

For this piece the printed fingering must be used in the examination.

Copyright © 2004 by Boosey & Hawkes Music Publishers Ltd.

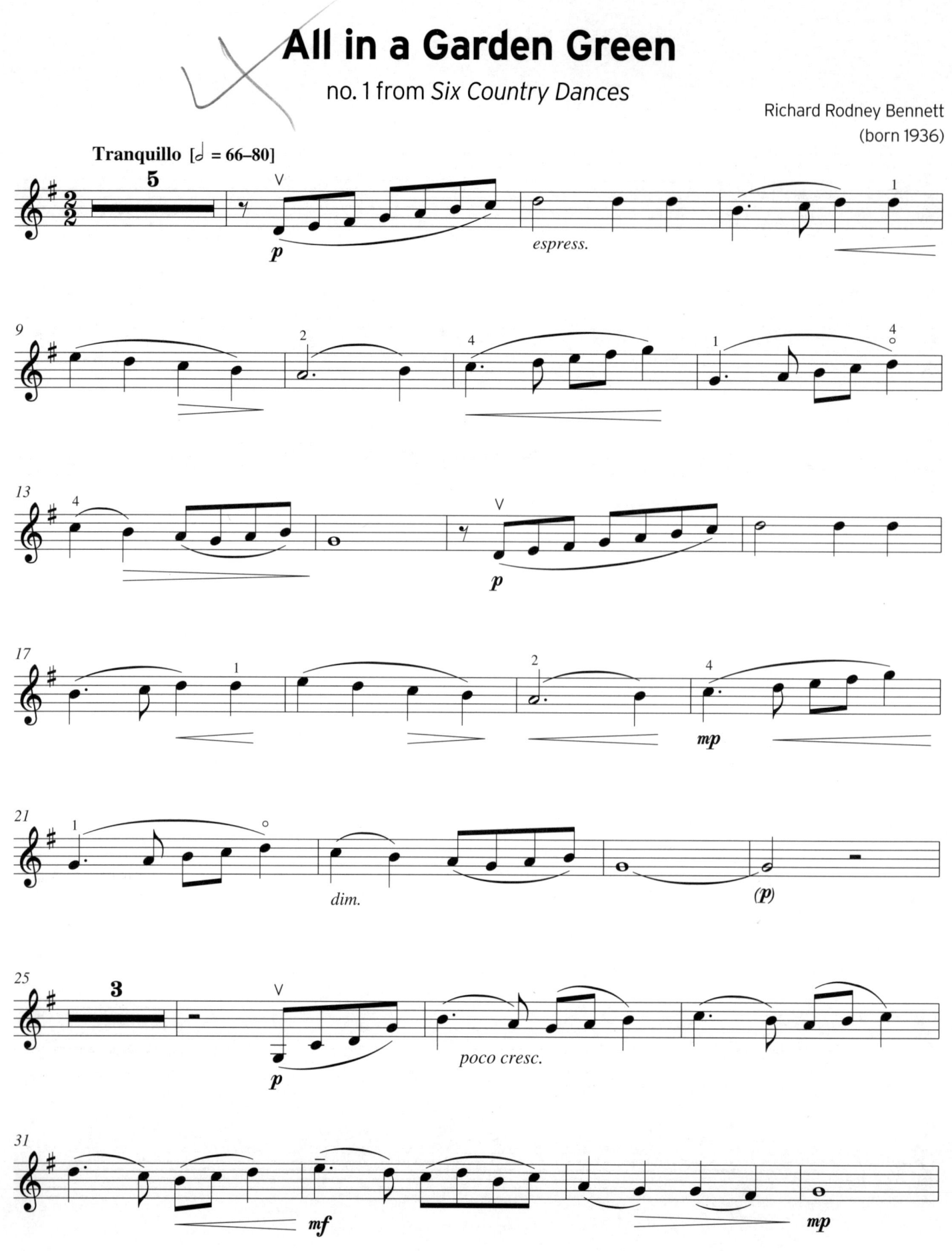

GROUP B

Flor de Yumuri

arr. Edward Huw Jones

Jorge Anckermann
(1877-1941)

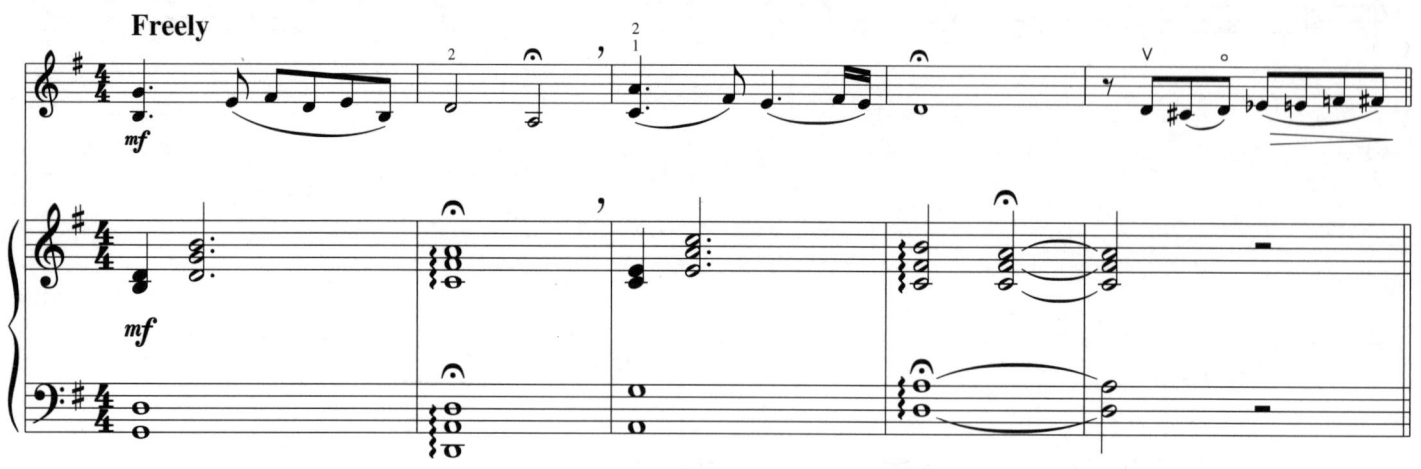

For this piece the printed fingering must be used in the examination.

16 Copyright © 2004 by Boosey & Hawkes Music Publishers Ltd.

I Got Rhythm

from *Girl Crazy*

George Gershwin (1898-1937)
and Ira Gershwin (1896-1983)

GROUP B

All in a Garden Green
no. 1 from *Six Country Dances*

Richard Rodney Bennett
(born 1936)

© Copyright 2003 Novello & Company Limited.
All Rights Reserved. International Copyright Secured. Used by permission.
(Sheet Music for *Six Country Dances* available from www.musicroom.com under item code NOV950600).

Melody

Claire Liddell

For this piece the printed fingering must be used in the examination.